Be Still and Know

A Collection of Inspirational Poetry
and Memorable Moments

Be Still and Know

A Collection of Inspirational Poetry
and Memorable Moments

Vickie Lathan McCorkle

illustrated by
Marilyn Pressley and Kelley Strong

iUniverse, Inc.
Bloomington

Be Still and Know
A Collection of Inspirational Poetry and Memorable Moments

iUniverse books may be ordered through booksellers or by contacting:

iUniverse
1663 Liberty Drive
Bloomington, IN 47403
www.iuniverse.com
1-800-Authors (1-800-288-4677)

ISBN: 978-1-4620-6209-6 (sc)
ISBN: 978-1-4620-6210-2 (hc)
ISBN: 978-1-4620-6211-9 (e)

Printed in the United States of America

Library of Congress Control Number: 2011961572

iUniverse rev. date: 11/29/2011

Dedication

This book is dedicated to my Uncle Henry Lathan.
He was an inspiration to all and lived a life sharing the
love of our Lord Jesus Christ. He was a wonderful
educator and he also enjoyed writing poetry.
In 1994 he published his book,
Henry and Pa Bill Just Talking.
Thank you
Uncle Henry for being my inspiration!

Words of wisdom from Henry Lathan:

Every day is a good day.
Any age is a good age.
Happiness is a state of mind,
which says…
Thank you God for your blessings
and I'm not going to want what
I can't afford.

"Uncle Henry"

Vickie Lathan McCorkle

Choices

(Dedicated to Uncle Henry)

God gives us opportunities and we must make a choice
He really wants to bless us but we must hear His voice
It's in the simple things each day
like how we treat someone
We can make the choice you see to call upon the Son
We'll never have the strength alone
to face this world each day
But life becomes a pleasure when we simply kneel to pray
And just because we're Christians
doesn't mean we know it all
We must seek to serve Him and rely upon His call
As we face our trials we can still show God is love
We must choose to find the blessings
sent by only God above
Our witness to the world you see
Comes not from what we say
It's in the choice that we can make to let Him have His way!

Thank you for your Christian witness.

I Love You Uncle Henry!

Choose you this day whom ye will serve;
But as for me and my house
we will serve the Lord. Joshua 24:15 KJV

Contents

Part I – A Collection of Inspirational Poetry

Part II – Memorable Moments

Illustrations

Photo Credits

My Porch
(About the Cover)

Artwork by Marilyn Pressley

On the porch I seem to find God's beauty can be found
It's there I find the simple pleasure of each and every sound.
You see the birds have found a home inside my fern so green
The flowers that surround us are the prettiest you've ever seen
I love to hear the chimes ring out as gentle breezes blow
The smell of fresh cut grass – the sweetest of all you know
Thank you God for solitude and time to spend with you
And for the time you give to rest with nothing much to do
The sweltering heat that summer brings simply seems to say
No other place I'd rather be than on MY porch today!

Acknowledgments

Marilyn Pressley graduated from Clemson University with a BA degree in Elementary Education. She also holds a Master's Degree in Elementary Education with a certification in art education. She lives in Lowrys, South Carolina and is a local elementary art teacher.

Kelley Strong is from Union, South Carolina and a graduate of Union County High School. There, she successfully developed her love of sports. She lettered in track, cross-country and wrestling. Kelley was recognized as the first female wrestler in Union County to win a match. During her senior year, Kelley was named 2011 Female Athlete of the Year. She received a scholarship to run cross country at Newberry College and plans to major in Biology.

Photo courtesy of PDPhoto.org

With God all things are possible.
Matthew 19:26 NIV

I would also like to thank my father, Cecil Lathan, for encouraging me to put this book of poetry together. He has been a great supporter and has spent countless hours memorizing and reciting my poetry.

With God, all things are possible! I hope God uses this book as a tool to encourage you through life's journey. May you find peace and comfort in day to day living with Jesus Christ.

Cecil M. Lathan

Foreword

by Joe Ann C. Dickson

In her first volume of original poems, Vickie Lathan McCorkle celebrates life, her love of God, family, and rich friendships. A central theme weaves these elements into a tapestry of beauty: Our world, created by Him, for His people, blended with our love and appreciation for His gifts, so freely given.

Out of Vickie's rich and full life, gratefulness shines from every page. We are here, not by chance, but by God's Divine Design! And our thanks to Him should be: "The Music of the spheres in His Heavenly, Eternal Ears!"

In her thoughtful poems, Vickie invites us to know our Creator, serve and honor Him, giving to others as He so freely gives to us. Will you take on this thought-provoking challenge in your life and relationships?

"Be Still and Know" is a series of journeys - through prayer, seasons of our lives, celebrations, family, parenting and honoring special people.

As you read, be prepared to travel! Vickie takes us on a memorable trip through South Carolina: from grandeur of the Blue Ridge Mountains to the "catch-your-breath" beauty of the Low Country's wide sandy beaches, Atlantic breezes, ocean waves, Palmetto palms, cities, towns and memorable folks.

A second poetic journey is the polar opposite: a wild trip with an Ant and friends: To Jerusalem! Cecil Lathan told this "Chronicle" to Vickie and her brother, Marion, when they were children, and still speaks it from memory!

Vickie's poem about Chester Park, where she teaches music, is now the School Song. Only one poem is "Advice": When you read "Be Ready" you will understand.

Not to be forgotten is "That Day" which revisits and returns to the unspeakable horror of September 11, 2001. May we read, remember and never forget…that day.

Your journey through Vickie's poetry will inspire, amuse and challenge you. I know, because I have read and re-read them. May you do the same, and be greatly blessed.

Mrs. Joe Ann Dickson

Vickie Lathan McCorkle

Preface

God works in mysterious ways. In the year 2000 I found myself wondering just what God was up to. I had no idea that during one of the most uncertain times of my life I would see God move in such a miraculous way. I was busy with the work I thought God wanted me to do. I taught elementary music all day, chorus before school, piano students after school and worked with a children's choir at a local church. Suddenly I became overwhelmed with the schedule and commitments I had made. One morning I noticed a sign on a marquee on the way to church. It read **"Be Still and Know that I am God."** I continued to see this sign for the next three months. I had no idea the sign was for me! My body was tiring and I was unable to keep the pace I had established for myself. I prayed and asked God to solve this problem however he saw fit. I did not know how to say no to anyone and my plate was piled way too high. Be careful what you ask for! God did solve my problem.

I lost my voice and knew it was more serious than just the typical laryngitis. After a visit with several specialists, I was told to sit quietly for months. That meant no school, chorus, piano, or church. WOW....I did not have any idea that was an option. Now just the thought of sitting at home and not speaking for several months somehow gave me a very uneasy feeling. I do not think I had ever been quiet for so long. Suddenly a peace came over me as I thought back to my prayer asking God to solve my problem. I knew without a doubt He was in charge. I had no idea what was about to happen. After three months the doctor discovered I had a cyst on my left vocal cord. This news certainly brought with it uncertainty because all music teachers need a voice. What would happen if the surgery did not go well? So many questions and very few answers and then without question, God spoke. It was Sunday and I had just settled in for my afternoon nap. I tossed and turned and finally dozed off.

And without warning, I woke up and knew I was to get a piece of paper and pen and write down what God was saying to me. I had never felt this type of urgency before. God had something to say and He had something to say to me! The first poem he spoke to me was **The Great Commission** followed by **Peace Within**. Now I knew why I was supposed to be quiet. God wanted to speak and I would have never heard Him in the fast-paced lifestyle I had created. The words God gave me brought great peace to my life. I gave in to this new God-given talent and continued hearing from God on a regular basis. This collection of poetry is nothing I did but only what **God did through me.** I count my blessings that God walked with me through the valley and brought me back to the mountain top. The surgery was successful and I returned to teaching and have taught for the past ten years with no problems. God gave back to me my love of music and also blessed me with a new talent. I pray these words will encourage you as you seek to find God's plan for your life.

I will sing unto the Lord, for he has been good to me.
Psalm 13:6 NIV 1984

Your Father knoweth what things you have need of,
before you ask Him.
Matthew 6:8 KJV

But my God shall supply all your need
according to His riches in glory
by Christ Jesus.
Philippians 4:19 KJV

Are You Listening?

Perhaps you've never thought about
how hard it'd really be
If the doctor's order given was to sit **silently**
You know we take for granted
simple things we do each day
We only seem to miss them when a trial comes our way
Now God I pray you'll help me as I strive to do your will
I know that something good will come if only I sit still
Sometimes you try to say
"My child, slow down and hear my call"
But often we keep going 'cause we seem to want it all
I never knew I'd find this gift of writing line by line
You see it really happened
when I stopped and took the time
Now friend I hope you'll listen as God calls you too to be
He wants us all to listen
Now we've finally found the *key!*

Be **still** and know that I am God.
Psalm 46:10 KJV

Part 1

A Collection of Inspirational Poetry

I Have a Plan

Photo courtesy of Melissa Lindsey

I Have a Plan for You

I never sought to find the answers on my own
Jesus said oh friend of mine
believe and won't you be strong
Listen to this song of mine
you'll know just who I am
For Christ has sent me to proclaim
He has for you a plan
I have a plan for you
it's simple as can be
Proclaim the name of Christ to men
and I will set you free

Come now my brothers, hear
what Christ has told us to do
Give your life to Christ and see
what a difference it makes in you
Sing of joy now, sing of gladness
sing of happiness too
For Christ has sent me to proclaim
He has a plan for you

I have a plan for you
it's simple as can be
Proclaim the name of Christ to men
and I will set you free

For I know the plans I have for you, declares the Lord,
Plans to prosper you and not to harm you,
plans to give you hope and a future.
Jeremiah 29: 11 KJV

Change My Heart, Oh, God

Change me like you, Lord, help me to stay
Close to you always, in every way
May others see Lord, compassion in me
As was our Savior, for all to see
Help mold my actions each day I pray
To better serve Thee through all that I say
Help me to sew kindness with all
And always remember on whom to call
Now Father guide me and send from above
Strength for today, to share of your love
Lord I am willing to serve you today
I pray that you'll send someone my way
To hear of your grace and what it can do
I pray that my life be an example of *You*

For it is by grace you have been saved through faith and
this is not from yourselves, it is a gift of God.
Ephesians 2:8 NIV

Verily I say unto you,
Except ye be converted,
And become as little children,
Ye shall not enter into the
kingdom of heaven.

Matthew 18:3b   KJV

Vickie Lathan McCorkle

The Great Commission

As the day comes to a close, I sit down with my pen
I ask the Lord to once again touch my heart and send
Someone with needs much greater than I could ever fill
But just a chance to share with them the story of my best friend
Just a chance to share today what Jesus means to me
I hope to never pass up the chance so all the world can see
He wants to be there every day to help us on our way
We all must learn to lean on Him and then we too may say
When Jesus comes into our heart He saves us from our sin
His grace is all sufficient for you my dearest friend
So as we're told, go out and tell of Him who died for you
To all of those around you just to name a few
The greatest news someone can hear will come from within your heart
It's not too late; today's the day, for all of us to start

Go ye therefore, and teach all nations, baptizing them in the
name of the Father, and of the Son, and of the Holy Ghost:
Teaching them to observe all things whatsoever
I have commanded you; and, lo, I am with you
always, even unto the end of the world.
Matthew 28: 19-20 KJV

Here I Am, Lord

As I sit and ponder the words I heard today
I think to myself, there must be a way
So many are hurting, in need of a friend
No one to turn to, so Christ you must send
Just someone to be there, encouraging along
Helps one to feel like they belong
It's me, I know Lord, you've asked me to say
Just a simple kind word, to someone today
I pray that my words will lighten their heart
And help them to see right from the start
We all face struggles from day to day
But somehow we make it if we will just *pray*
Lord, help me to find someone today
That's hurting inside and maybe won't say
I don't know the problem, but this I can say
Lord, I'll be there for someone today

And let us consider how we may spur one another on
toward love and good deeds.
Let us not give up meeting together,
as some are in the habit of doing,
but let us encourage one another
and all the more as you see the Day approaching.
Hebrews 10: 24-25 NIV 1984

Daily thoughts and reflections....................

_____

_____

_____

_____

_____

_____

_____

_____

_____

_____

_____

_____

_____

_____

_____

A Single Light

As we look around us, in the world today
We find a world of darkness and with it comes dismay
As we self examine what God would have us do
We must start within ourselves and to the closest few
A single light can change the dark from what may seem dismay
But this one light can change a heart and then we all may say
A heart for God can change the world if on Christ we shall depend
No longer will the darkness fill our world with constant sin
We must seek to find someone each and every day
A little help to just someone may go a long, long way
It's quite an easy way to start to turn from dark to light
It's time we take a stand for God with just A Single Light

For you were once darkness,
but now you are light in the Lord.
Ephesians 5:8 NIV 1984

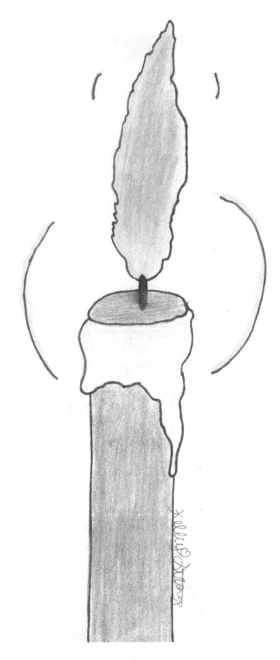

"A Single Light"

I Count It All A Blessing

Sometimes God works in ways unseen, we often wonder why
He takes us through uncertainties, now on Him we must rely
You see we can't begin to know the whats and whys and when
But our God is in charge, He'll choose you too, to send
Once we choose to do God's will the tests will surely come
Sometimes we even question who the tests are from
But God has great and mighty plans to use us all you see
The test will help to make us strong and be more like Thee
God wants to mold and make us clean to follow Him each day
No matter what the trial, I thank Him as I pray
I look to see what I can learn; God leads me through each day
I'm sure God wants to bless us all and teach us how to pray
You see our God will sometimes close a door along the way
This will help us lean on Him and what He has to say
We never know what's up ahead but God sees everything
I guess that's why we trust Him and praise Him as we sing
I thank you God for strength today to pass this test for You
I pray in all your wisdom, I'll know just what to do!

I Count It All A Blessing

We do not enjoy being disciplined. It is painful at the
time, but later, after we have learned from it, we have peace,
because we start living the right way.
Hebrews 12:11 NCV

Good News

Today I'd like to share with you the greatest news I've heard
I found it hidden deep within the pages of God's word
You see many years have passed and we still act the same
We go to church, read God's word and even praise His name
But something is missing when that's all we say and do
The Great Commission has been sent to both me and you
God wants us to be willing to tell what He has done
To share the love He had for us by sending His own son
The world if filled with hurting souls that know not of His grace
It's up to us to tell the world He died to take our place
God has a plan for all of us if we will only say
Lord, I am willing, please use me today!
Please send someone who needs to hear of joy, peace and love
And give me the strength I need from only you above
I know I'll never be the same; I've shared you with a friend
And thank you for the strength you give until the very end

For if you tell others with your own mouth
that Jesus Christ is your Lord
and believe in your own heart
that God has raised Him from the dead,
you will be saved.
Romans 10:9 TLB

Sunrise at Springmaid Beach on
Memorial Day 2011

Peace Within

As I come to the ocean for a short reprieve
It's here that God makes it easy for one to believe
The waters seem endless, no boundary in sight
I know that my God will make everything right
I listen to the ocean and feel the gentle breeze
I know that peace within me comes from what God sees
The future is all planned out; it's He who holds my hand
He only wants us to trust Him and take a mighty stand
When despair and uncertainties come our way once more
We all must remember that He will open the door
What may seem an ending, can be a brand new start
But first we must trust Him and let Him into our heart
What joy He gives through every trial, a peace now from within
I pray today that I will see what my God wants to send
I pray I find the blessings in each and every day
I pray that my God help me in every word I say
I thank Him for the good times and for the trials too
I thank Him for being my Savior and knowing just what to do

Rejoice in the Lord always
and again I say, Rejoice!
Philippians 4:4 NIV

Be anxious for nothing but in everything
by prayer and supplication with thanksgiving
let your requests be made known to God.
And the peace of God, which passeth all understanding,
shall guard your hearts and minds through Christ Jesus.
Philippians 4:6-7 NKJV

Just One Day?

It's Sunday morning; "We must get up"
I heard my Mama say
It seems a shame we only get up this one day to pray
I guess God knows that some will say
"This is the day to pray"
But I myself wonder why just one day to pray
I know God must miss us all during the week
I guess he gets lonely until His face we seek
Sometimes we forget our burdens He wants to share
We try to fix each problem, when our Father is always there
Our problem seems too big or we hate to bother Him
We always make excuses until our light goes dim
Now times are rough, we can't go on, so now to Him we turn
It's such a shame it takes all this for each of us to learn
God wants to hear from us each day just like our closest friend
He wants to share the good times and help our hearts to mend
Now when we depend on Him our lives are truly blessed
It's He that gives us comfort and in Him we find true rest

Delight yourself in the Lord;
and He will give you the desires of your heart.
Psalm 37:4 NIV

Don't Take It for Granted

Sometimes we take for granted the pleasures of each day
We give it little thought you see as we are on our way
Too busy in the morning to notice those around
We like it nice and quiet with very little sound
Our mind begins to cover the things we'll do today
We rarely even notice just what our children say
We spend so little time with God to thank Him as we pray
It seems we barely notice the routine of today
We take for granted those who care and always fill our needs
But what a joy to take the time to plant a tiny seed
You see life's greatest pleasures come from looking right around
It's really in our family, true joy can now be found

> Whoever sows sparingly will also reap sparingly,
> and whoever sows generously
> will also reap generously.
> 2 Corinthians 9:6 NIV

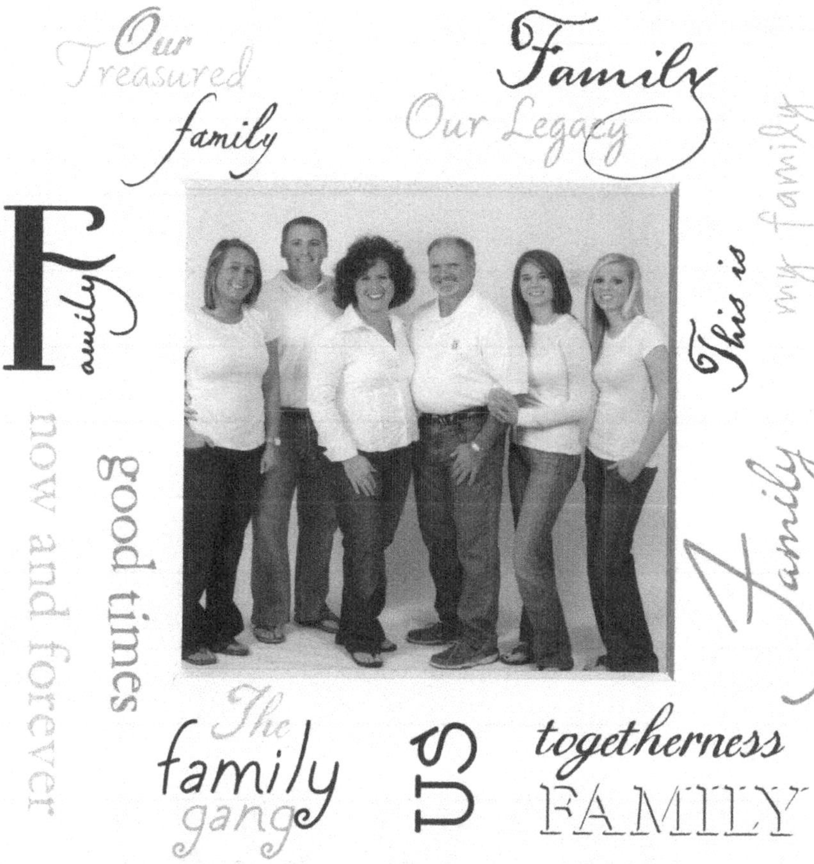

Our
Treasured
family

Family
Our Legacy

This is my family

Family

now and forever

good times

The family gang

US

togetherness
FAMILY

Thank God for your blessings and list ways you can be a
blessing to someone.........

_____

_____

_____

_____

_____

_____

_____

_____

_____

_____

_____

_____

_____

_____

_____

Thank You

Father, we thank you for blessing us today
And thank you for giving us the words you'd have us say
Thank you for Jesus, who died to take our place
And for the way you love us with your amazing grace
Thank you for the simple things we sometimes fail to see
Help to keep us mindful and focused just on Thee
Thank you for the guidance you give when we are still
And help us always strive to live within your Holy will
Thank you for our family and friends who mean so much
Help us show each one your love through just a simple touch
Thank you for your spirit of joy and peace and love
And help us lift our voices to only *You* above
Thank you for the gift of song and for a way to share
Just how much you mean to us and just how much you care
May we be a blessing to some lost soul today
And may the light of Jesus help them find their way

This is the day the Lord has made,
let us rejoice and be glad in it.
Psalm 118:24 NIV

I'm not the potter …
I'm just a piece of clay.

Who's In Charge?

Although sometimes I must admit I like to be in charge
I find it's less important that I become the Sarg.
Someone to boss and tell each day the things they need to do
I guess it's really not my place; it's all up to You
It sure is less hectic when I'm in charge of me
No worries about the others, just trying to see
What God has planned for me and for the others too
I'm sure He'll reveal to us just what to do
I'm not the potter or the wheel; I'm just a piece of clay
I know my Savior's loving hand will guide me on my way
You see I've learned a lot from Him through each and every day
I'm not in charge of you or me, its God who's boss today

Trust in the Lord with all your heart
and lean not on your own understanding;
in all your ways acknowledge Him and
He shall direct your paths.
Proverbs 3:5-6 NKJV

Be Ready

Please excuse the way I look, I know I seem a mess
If I had known you'd come today, I'd have shopped for a new dress
I'd clean my house; I'd make the beds
I'd cook your favorite meal
I guess you'd think this all was great, I wonder how you'd feel
It seems a shame we never know the day you're coming back
It looks as if we're not prepared; we even seem to lack
The knowledge of your saving grace when you so plainly said
Just open up your Bible and read your daily bread
It seems so clear to live each day as if it were our last
You want to save us from our sin and wipe away our past
So listen now my friend you see, be ready every day
'Cause only God above knows when He'll come to pass this way

And He will appear a second time,
not to bear sin but to bring salvation to
those who are waiting for Him.
Hebrews 9:28 NIV

God's Snow

Today it snowed and snowed some more, a sight we rarely see
The snowflakes fell from everywhere; they even fell on me
With frozen feet and runny nose I tried to lend a hand
We must build this snowman, but how can we make him stand?
We built him from the fallen snow, so pure and white and clean
We thought the finished product was the cutest you've ever seen
The snow God sent for all of us was quite a sight to see
It covered each and every thing, even the tallest tree
This tree was a beauty with snow on every limb
It was a simple wonder, sent to us by only Him

Stand still and consider the wondrous works of God.
Job 37:14 KJV

GOD'S SNOW

Photo courtesy of Pam Wilson

Mrs. Jo Ann Wishert
"My Friend"

To Thank You

God's given us another day, there's beauty all around
It's when we take the time to look that beauty can be found
You see so much you've rarely seen although it's been right there
Sometimes it takes an act of God before we learn to care
It seems we found the joy in things we felt we had to do
But now, you see, our joy is found in spending time with you
It means so much to have a friend on whom you can rely
The simple little things you did to share a friendly "Hi"
The cards, the calls, the gifts you sent were thoughtful as can be
But thank you most of all for prayers you lifted up for me
The days go by and stronger still my body seems to be
I know my God is in control; He wants the best for me
I thank God now for friends like you who show they really care
Your friendship means the world to me
It's nice to know you're there

A merry heart doeth good like a medicine,
but a broken spirit drieth the bones.
Proverbs 17:22 KJV

Without Complaining

I'd like to think the day would come when everyone could find
Something nice to talk about, I know you wouldn't mind
There's always something good in one if only we will seek
You've given all a special gift and even to the weak
We can find the best you see in all that comes our way
It's simple if we think of what Christ would have us say
Now some are looking just to find a problem every day
Their joy comes from arguing with anything you say
Our days will be much happier when pleasant things we say
God gives us all a choice to make each and every day
So as you look for things to say, I know that you will find
Good things come to those who wait and never seem to mind
I pray we'll always find the best in what we say and do
But most of all, I pray dear God
We choose to follow *You.*

Do everything without complaining or arguing,
so that you may become blameless and pure, children of God.
Philippians 2: 14-15 NIV

Do. Everything. Without. Complaining

God's Love Seeds

As I plant a seed today, I hope to see it grow
I'll do the simple things I can before I have to go
You know we have a chance to sow God's love in all we do
I pray we choose to touch the lives if only of a few
It's really very simple if we try to find each day
A smile to share with those around as if we want to say
God loves you and we all must share this message with a friend
Just simply open up your heart and Christ will enter in
God gives a light to each of us to shine for Him each day
It's when we give away our joy that blessings come our way
We may not think our seeds have grown but we don't have to see
It's just my job to plant the seed my God has given *me*!

I planted the seed, Apollos watered it,
but God made it grow.
So neither he who plants nor he who waters is anything,
but only God, who makes things grow.
1 Corinthians 3: 6-7 NIV

Zachary McCorkle

Look Around

Today I shopped for flowers and it seemed so hard to choose
With rows and rows of colors, I didn't know which to use
The brilliance of each flower and the brightness of the sun
Seem to add to days of leisure and having lots of fun
Each day is filled with beauty as the grass begins to grow
The splendor of the springtime helps our hearts to overflow
So as God brings this joy to all, so little can compare
With the beauty all around us and the freshness of the air

Another Day

Thank you for the sunrise, the beauty of this day
Thank you for another chance to worship you and pray
Outside the birds sing out to all the sounds we love to hear
Another day God's given us without a single fear
God cares for each and every bird; He meets their every need
He wants to care for each of us if on His Word we'll feed
No worries or concerns you see, for what the future holds
'Cause each new day I try my best to do what I am told
The Bible helps us see God's face; it helps us know He cares
It tells of how Christ died for us and how our sin He bears
Now thank you God for one more day to look around and see
The simple beauty of this day and grace you've given me

Look at the birds of the air; they do not sow or reap or
store away in barns,
And yet your heavenly Father feeds them.
Are you not much more valuable than they?
Matthew 6:26 NIV

Our Gift

Sometimes we think we can't do much, when really we are blessed
You see the gift God gave to us is not just like the rest
God's given out the things he needs for all of us to do
And many times we find a gift that seems to be brand new
It's such a joy to find the gift God's given us to use
But we must find within our hearts this special gift to choose
By grace these gifts God chose to give are sent from up above
It's up to us to use our gifts to share our Savior's love
Now when we find we're serving Him and striving every day
We'll find the joy of living, no matter what some may say

We have different gifts, according to the grace given us.
Romans 12:6 NIV

Seize the Moment

So many people fail to find
happiness is a state of mind

We can't plan to enjoy the day
only when things go our way

Each day brings true happiness
if we will choose to find the best

We can wait to be happy one day
or enjoy ourselves along the way

No matter what the circumstance
choose to free your heart to dance

Life's pleasures then you'll find each day
and strength to enjoy all things I pray

No more waiting, real joy you'll find
just always remember it's a state of mind!

Happy is the man who findeth wisdom, and the man
that getteth understanding for the gain from it is better than
gain from silver and the profit thereof than fine gold.
Proverbs 3:13-14 ASV

Cozmel, Mexico

My Favorite Things

Today I choose to think about the things that bring me joy
Like living with a sweet and cute teenage boy
I love the sound of baseball games and how they make me feel
It seems I have no worries and nothing seems too real
You can't turn back the time, you see
Each day you must select
The simple little things today on which you can reflect
There's nothing like the memories made, we have no second chance
So lighten up, enjoy today and teach your heart to dance
I can't imagine eating out at any other place
You see, *The Front Porch* knows my name and can't forget my face
My favorite things like fresh fried squash, I'd offer everyday
But no one seems to listen to what I have to say
I love the fellowship of friends and what they mean to me
The time we spend together, one can clearly see
Each one has touched my life and I am truly blessed
I thank God every day for friends; I know I have the best
I also love the way I feel when floating on the pool
You'll never find a better way to keep your body cool
And let me mention Mom and Dad who always seem to care
The love they have for me you see is something very rare
Now I could never go without the mention of my church
West End Baptist is the place you'll never have to search
For people who are friendly and who love to see your face
It's nice to feel God's loving grace in such a wondrous place
I don't guess I have to say that music is my thing
But lately all the doctors say "Be quiet and don't sing"
But that's o.k. 'cause I still know that music's all around
Just listen to the beauty of each and every sound
I guess the children's laughter and the way they make me feel
Will always keep me smiling with a joy that's very real
I pray I never lose the joy that comes from *favorite things*
And help me God to always see what pleasure *you* can bring

Parasailing in the Bahamas

Retirement

Written for Brenda Cabrey

God's given us a brand new day
Our lives won't be the same

So much has changed along the way
Since the day you came

You see your joy from deep within was shared with those around
It always seemed impossible to find you feeling down

The little extra things you did meant more than words can say
The smile you shared with everyone brightened up our day

Now things won't be quite the same when you're not here next year
We'll hold the memories we've all made within our hearts so dear

Now, rest, relax, enjoy yourself and thank God everyday
'Cause he has truly blessed *you* in each and every way

Thank you for your commitment to The Chester County School District
You will always be remembered

Seasons

Winter

Winter shows just how powerful it can be
It sometimes leaves us without electricity
Winter can bring the most beautiful sight
A snow-laden tree on a wintry night

Spring

Spring is a season that one just longs to feel
The sight and smell of this season is something very real
The temperature is perfect and we feel the need to clean
The blossoms that surround us are the prettiest you've ever seen

Summer

Summer brings vacation and a time we've waited for
Even though our days are longer, we seem to long for more
Summer brings fresh vegetables served with a glass of sweet tea
But the heat that comes with summer is sometimes too hot for me

Fall

Fall adds color to every tree around
The leaves begin to fall and soon they'll cover the ground
Football, friends and family all add a special touch
Each season is a wonder: God's given us so much

There is a time for everything
and a season
for every activity under heaven.
Ecclesiastes 3:1 NIV

Daytona Beach, 2010

Jesus first
Others second
Yourself last

God Is Love

Written for Mrs. Linda Wylie

I learned this verse so long ago, I think right from the start
It's the kind of verse you place down deep within your heart
Now just three words, how can it be?
That they could change us all
But when you give your life to Christ you listen to His call
Each day we strive to live for Him, we try to show His love
But each new day we bow and pray for strength from up above
You see in every circumstance we get the chance to show
What our Savior means to us and just what we know
Now God is love, I guess we all should practice this each day
Sometimes it's hard and we forget to think before we say
The way we speak or how we act or treat someone, you see,
Should really be the way our God would treat you or me
Now those three words can change one's life,
I know how it changed me
I pray the world will feel God's love and choose to follow Thee

> Whoever does not love does not know God,
> because God is love.
> 1 John 4:8 NIV

Share God's Love

Think of a way that you can say "I Love You" today
Think of someone who needs to hear a kind word you have to say
Think of how you feel when someone calls you just to say
"Hello, I miss you and I'm thinking of you today"
Think of a surprise that would brighten up a friend
Maybe they just need to know on whom they can depend
Think of how it makes you feel to get a hug or two
And surely you remember what a simple hug can do
Love is a gift to be given every day
This gift of love is greatest when we give it away
Let's set our minds on things to do and ways to share our love
It all begins when we receive God's love from up above

> You shall love the Lord your God with all your heart,
> with all your soul and with all your mind.
> This is the first and great commandment.
> And the second is like it.
> You shall love your neighbor as yourself.
> Matthew 22:37-39 NKJV

"My Sweet Cousin"
Lori Finch Waldrep

The Joy of Easter

Though Easter comes but once a year, so many have been told
This day of celebration is one to behold!
Our Savior died upon the cross to take our sin away
No greater gift could any give than what He gave that day
You see they placed Him in a tomb, no thought of His return
It's really quite amazing how much they had to learn
In three short days Christ rose again, now how could that be?
You see He died and rose again that we might be free
He asked that we believe in Him and what He did that day
And as we ask Him in our hearts we simply must pray
God wants to share His love with us and give us peace within
And through this Easter story, I hope that you'll begin
To see the cross and what it means to each of us today
I pray somehow we'll never forget the price He had to pay

My command is this: Love each other as I have loved you.
Greater love has no one than this,
that he lay down his life for his friends.
John 15:12-13 NIV

Why The Cross?

It was God's plan that Christ would die upon the cross that day
He'd give up His only son just to make a way
Salvation comes but with a cost
A price paid long ago
Christ gave His life upon the cross
So each of us would know
God wants to save each one of us
No need for us to pay
We first believe, confess our sins
And let Him have his way
So when you see a cross hung high
A symbol of God's great plan
I hope you stop and think about
This gift from God to Man

God so loved the world
that He gave his only begotten son,
that whosoever believeth in Him
Should not perish but have everlasting life.
John 3:16 KJV

A Mother's Love

God's given each a MOTHER, no one ever can replace
The bond you share together or the smile upon her face
As years go by her words seem wise, we too can truly say
God's given us an awesome job to guide along the way
Our children bring us joy in ways we simply can't express
They always seem to bless us even though we get no rest
A mother always looks for ways to brighten up your day
It's in the little things she does and what she has to say
I guess we'll never grow too old for mother's tender touch
I pray she knows the love she gives will never be too much

Train up a child in the way he should go
and when he is old,
he will not depart from it.
Proverbs 22:6 KJV

I Love You Zachary Leigh McCorkle

Margaret Louise Cassels Lathan
My Mom

Vickie Lathan McCorkle

Single Mom

Sometimes I think how nice it'd be if there were two of us
But since there's only one you see, it all becomes a must
No job's too big, it must be done, I think this job's for me
I'll try to make our house a home, that really is the key
You see, sometimes we feel alone, we even question "when"
But life's a journey we must take and learn from where we've been
No one or place can fill the void you have inside your heart
It's only when Christ enters in that you'll begin to start
Now you'll see the joy in life comes really from within
I know my God has blessed me so with many, many friends
Each one adds something new to each and every day
And thank you God for sending them to bless along the way
I face a brand new day and pray God helps me see today
But most of all I pray for strength to let *Him* have his way

> But they that wait upon the Lord
> shall renew their strength.
> Isaiah 40:31 KJV

Happy Father's Day

Happy Father's Day to you, I hope your day's the best
Of all the fathers in the world, I'd choose YOU from the rest
No one could ever measure up, 'cause you surpass them all
You're a Dad who's always there when I seem to call
God's given you a gift, you see, you have a special touch
The way you treat those around really means so much
Now "Thank You Dad" for raising me and helping me to see
The world can be a better place when it begins with *me*

I Love You

And whoever trusts in the Lord,
happy is he.
Proverbs 16:20 NKJY

HAPPY FATHER'S DAY

That Day in September

September 11, 2001

We'll never forget that day in September
Our lives have been changed and we'll always remember
The horror, the grief, the disbelief
Hours of anguish with no relief
Each time I hear a plane go by, I stop and think and wonder why
How could someone hate us so?
I guess that's one thing we'll never know

Once standing tall against the sky
Who'd have thought one day we'd cry
To see those towers crumbling down
With few survivors ever found
How could life end in such a way
When innocent people had to pay
They went to work just like before
But we won't see them any more

Our hearts are broken, we feel such pain
And just what has this one man gained?
He's taken mothers, fathers and children too
And left behind so much to do

God bless this land! Heal its people that we might stand
Together, united, as never before
And may we learn to depend on You more
I pray for wisdom and guidance each day
And may we guard the words we say
America needs you! May we always remember
you can guide us through that day in September

> If my people, who are called by my name,
> will humble themselves and pray
> and seek my face and turn from their wicked ways,
> then will I hear from heaven and will forgive their sin
> and will heal their land.
> 2 Chronicles 7:14 NKJV

God's Blessings

Today God brings a blessing, the freedom that we share
So many take for granted, while others find it rare
It's living in a country where Christ is still our King
And little children's voices bring blessings as they sing
So many fight for freedom, they fight for you and me
They give their lives if needed, to keep our country free
We thank you God for these dear ones who keep us safe and strong
We pray you bring protection so nothing else goes wrong
Now bless their families with your peace
And keep them safe this day
Give them reassurance that an end is on the way
So long ago you sent Your Son, a blessing brought that day
And He would pay the greatest price by giving us a way
For freedom not just for today but freedom that will last
In Christ we find that freedom when He forgives us of our past
Help us Lord to look today for blessings all around
Help us find that peace and joy in each and every sound

If we confess our sins,
He is faithful and just to forgive us our sins
and to cleanse us from all unrighteousness.
1 John 1:9 KJV

Proud of Our Veterans

Thanksgiving

Thanksgiving is a time for family and friends
It's the special time we share our feelings from within
Just the thought of giving thanks, so much to thank God for
But often we forget our thanks and still God blesses more
Each day there is beauty if we only try to see
It's the heart of gratitude that really is the key
As we start each morning, may we ask God up above
To help us in our daily walk to share His wondrous love
And may we always realize today could be the best
Let's not forget to thank our God and He'll provide the rest
Faith, hope and happiness come not from worldly things
I pray we all experience the peace true joy can bring
Thank you God for giving me a voice to sing and pray
And for the joy to laugh and talk with words you'd have me say
Thank you for this country and may we simply say
Thank you God for giving us another Thanksgiving Day

Make a joyful noise unto the Lord, all ye lands.
Serve the Lord with gladness;
come before his presence with singing.
Know ye that the Lord he is God;
it is he that hath made us and not we ourselves;
we are his people and the sheep of his pasture.
Enter into his gates with thanksgiving
and into his courts with praise;
be thankful unto him, and bless his name.
For the Lord is good;
his mercy is everlasting
and his truth endureth to all generations.
Psalm 100 KJV

Kristen Lathan Moss and Zack McCorkle

Proud to Be An American

Robin Page Weeks

The Family

Merry Christmas

May we celebrate the birth of He who came that day
And may we live our life for Christ in everything we say
We share a Merry Christmas with everyone around
But in this Merry Christmas, can our Christ be found?
We shop for the perfect gift, we gather with our friends
We think of those who mean the most and choose a card to send
We plan each Christmas party, so no one feels left out
And surely those around us know what Christmas is about
But do we share our Jesus, who came that day to show
The love of God within us, He wants the world to know

The angels sang of *His* great birth, the shepherds gathered 'round
This was a day to celebrate, our Savior had been found
Now Jesus lived and died for us to save us from our sin
And when we open up our hearts, He'll surely enter in
Now as we celebrate this year, the gift of Christ you see
No greater gift could any give than Christ has given me

And the angel said unto them, "Fear not; for, behold,
I bring you good tidings of great joy,
which shall be to all people.
For unto you is born this day in the city of David a Savior,
which is Christ the Lord."
Luke 2:10-11 KJV

A Christmas Wish Come True

A wish, it's true, can come to me or you
A hope, a dream, is much more than it seems
A change, new ways, not done just like before
A family, a friend, a simple note to send
A time to share, a time for being there
A smile, a kiss, you surely shouldn't miss
A chance to say I love you everyday
A heart that fills the simple wish for one
The peace, the joy, the hope of girls and boys
A gift, a tree, a star that shines so bright
A simple wish that's made on Christmas night
A wish is sent, this Christmas wish to you
May the magic of the season be your Christmas wish come true

But those who hope in the Lord will renew their strength.
They will soar on wings like eagles;
they will run and not grow weary,
They will walk and not be faint.
Isaiah 40:31 NIV

Glory to God in the highest, and on earth peace,
goodwill toward men.
Luke 2:14 KJV

In memory of Reenie Crabtree Lathan Foster
who lost her battle with cancer January 21, 2011

Coming Home

Home is the heart of those that dwell within

Home is the joy of spending time with friends

Home brings us close to share what's on our mind

Home brings us peace, that's sometimes hard to find

Home is the place where love is always found

Home is even knowing every tiny sound

Home is the smell of cider simmering slow

Home is your favorite meal your Mom just seems to know

Home is each memory you've made throughout the years

Home is the place you've cried and shared many tears

Home is the Christmas tree, adorned with white clean snow

Home's the smell of candles sitting neatly in a row

Home's the family Bible and how we live each day

Home's the tone of voice we use and words we have to say

Home is where my Christ lives, a place of peace and rest

Home is simply knowing He provides the Very Best!

Merry Christmas to You
and May Christ
Fill Your Home This Season

Foote Street

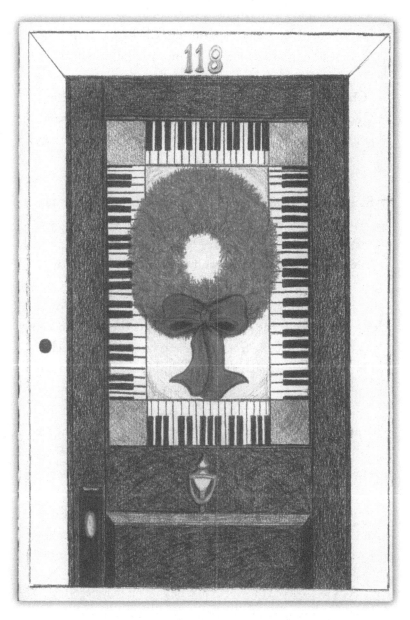

Artwork by Marilyn Pressley

The Greatest Gift

Candles glowing, ribbons flowing, wreaths on every door
Hearts are filled with laughter, who could ask for any more?
Snowflakes falling, friends are calling, Christmas time is near
A time of reassurance of the ones you hold so dear

Children singing, bells ringing, excitement stirs within
God chose this special time of year, His only Son to send
Lights glimmering, cider simmering, a celebration is at hand
The little baby Mary knew did grow to be a man

Simple living, endless giving, He'd bear the cross one day
And then He'd send His spirit to guide us on our way
Peace, joy and love He gives to all who come His way
It's really hard to understand the price He had to pay

Families caring, hearts sharing, Christmas trees aglow
God's precious gift He sent to us, He wants the world to know
His saving grace so freely given, no one can buy or sell
He simply asks we share His love and find someone to tell

Salvation is the greatest gift, the only gift for me
It's not wrapped with fancy paper or placed beneath the tree
It's given out of love by the one who took my place
And one day I'll see my Savior and look into His face

Thank you God for Jesus, born simply out of love
And thank you for our blessings that flow from heav'n above

For God so loved the world, that he gave his only begotten
Son,
that whosoever believeth in Him, should not perish,
but have everlasting life.
John 3:16 KJV

To MANKIND: From GOD
Artwork by Marilyn Pressley

Write a thank you card to those people in your life who have helped make you who you are..........

_____

_____

_____

_____

_____

_____

_____

_____

_____

_____

_____

_____

_____

_____

_____

Rejoice

One starry night so long ago with haste the shepherds came
To see the baby Mary knew, Jesus would be His name
God sent this tiny baby, so precious as could be
He'd come to save this world, you see, and sinners just like me

Rejoice, the time has come, a Savior has been born!
Rejoice, let's celebrate on this Christmas morn

Now, Mary didn't know why God had chosen her that day
And most of all she didn't know the price He'd have to pay
But in her heart she knew this child was sent from God above
And He had come to show us how to share God's wondrous love

Rejoice, the time has come, a Savior has been born!
Rejoice, let's celebrate on this Christmas morn

So many years have come and gone, but Jesus is the same
And miracles still happen at the mention of His name
And Christ will take away your sin, you simply need to say:
"I choose to give my life to Christ and let Him have His way"

Rejoice, the time has come, a Savior has been born!
Rejoice, let's celebrate on this Christmas morn

Rejoice! Rejoice! A Savior has been born!

And they came with haste,
and found Mary, and Joseph, and the babe lying in a manger.
Luke 2:16 KJV

Part II

Memorable Moments

To God Be the Glory!

To My Son

On the sixteenth day of November in 1983
God chose to send the greatest gift that he could send to me
His hair was blonde; his eyes were blue
His skin was light and fair
I knew the love I felt for him was something very rare
You see, God knew that from that day our lives would grow to be
A special kind of love to share for all the world to see
Now joy this baby brought to me, a peace down deep within
I knew it was the Savior's love on whom I must depend
Now as the years passed on, you see, we two could smile and say
We share a love God gave to us no one can take away
I must admit I'm mighty proud of what I see today
I have a Son who strives to please in each and every way
His heart is kind, his words are wise and love he gives to all
He always seems to be there when someone needs to call
I hope he knows no other love could ever replace
The greatest love he'll always find upon his Mother's face
Now to my son, I hope you know, this bond we share today
Is only strong because, in love, we both learned how to pray

Behold, children are a gift of the Lord.
Psalm 127: 3a NASB
Discipline your son,
and he will give you peace;
He will bring delight to your soul.
Proverbs 29: 17 NIV

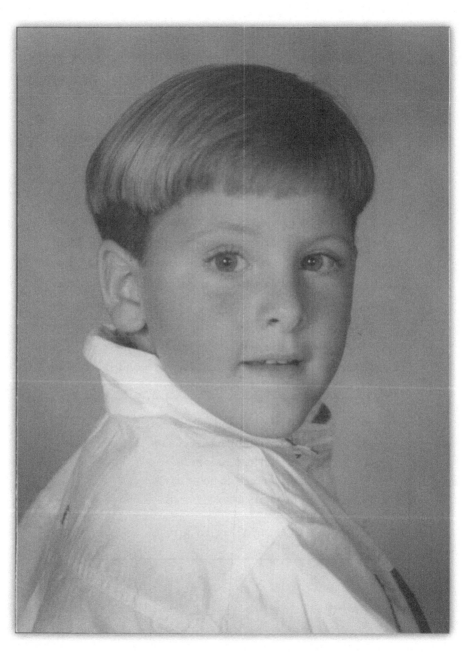

Zachary Leigh McCorkle

I Honor Thee

To My Mom
Margaret Louise Cassels Lathan

Today's the day I honor one who cared for all my needs
She's the one who helped me grow from a tiny seed
I guess she often wondered what I would grow to be
I know deep down within her heart she hoped I'd honor Thee
I knew she was quite proud of me, my job, my house, my Son
She often looked at me and said, "I'm proud of you: Well done!"
But not until my heart was changed and everything made clear
The things that meant so much to me seem not to be so dear
I hope you see my purpose now to honor Thee each day
I pray, Lord, you will help me be a servant everyday
No job, no house, nor family can ever replace
The gift God gave to each of us, his son and wondrous grace

Her children arise and call her blessed;
her husband also,
and he praises her:
Many women do noble things,
but you surpass them all.

Proverbs 31: 28-29 NIV

Margaret Louise Cassels Lathan

Cecil Marion Lathan

My Dad

I guess sometimes we wonder what a Dad should really be
I've got a good example in the Father sent to me!
They're big and strong, with lots of hair and seem to know it all
They want to hear from us each day, so we better call
They know our needs and seem to find the words we need to hear
It's in our Dad we put our trust and learn not to fear
A Dad loves you when he knows a dress is the best thing
To buy this dress, he'll sell his cows or do most anything
He'll never fully understand the things girls like to do
But this doesn't matter 'cause I know his love is true
A Dad drops by unannounced: he wants to check on you
He often brings you vegetables and tells you what to do!
A Dad has a way, you see he teaches us each day
It's really how you treat someone and what you have to say
It's easier to find the best in all we say and do
A Dad is proud no matter what he's always proud of you
Now God I'd like to thank you for the Dad you sent my way
My heart is filled and this you know I really want to say
In all the world I couldn't find a better Dad you see
'Cause all in all, He's the *best*, He's the Dad for *me!*

Happy is the man that findeth wisdom,
and the man that gains understanding.
Proverbs 3: 13 NKJV

The Little Ant Going to Jerusalem

(My Dad's favorite folktale)

Once upon a time, there was a little ant going to Jerusalem
He fell in the snow, and broke his paw
He said, **"Oh, snow, how strong you are**,
to break the paw of a little ant going to Jerusalem."
The snow said, "The sun who melts me is stronger than I,"
Oh, sun, how strong you are, to melt the snow,
that breaks the paw of a little ant going to Jerusalem.
The sun said, "The clouds that cover me are stronger than I,"
Oh, clouds how strong you are, to cover the sun,
that melts the snow,
that breaks the paw of a little ant going to Jerusalem.
The clouds said, "The wind that moves me is stronger than I."
Oh, wind how strong you are, to move the clouds, that cover the sun,
that melts the snow,
that breaks the paw of a little ant going to Jerusalem.
The wind said, "The mountain that stops me is stronger than I."
Oh, mountain, how strong you are, to stop the wind,
that moves the clouds,
that cover the sun, that melts the snow,
that breaks the paw of a little ant going to Jerusalem;
The mountain said, "The rat that bores me is stronger than I."
Oh, rat how strong you are, to bore the mountain,
that stops the wind,
that moves the clouds, that cover the sun, that melts the snow,
that breaks the paw of a little ant going to Jerusalem.
The rat said, "The cat who eats me is stronger than I."
Oh, cat how strong you are, to eat the rat, that bores the mountain, that
stops the wind, that moves the clouds,
that cover the sun, that melts the snow,
that breaks the paw of a little ant going to Jerusalem.
The cat said, "The dog that chases me is stronger than I."
Oh, dog how strong you are, to chase the cat,
that eats the rat, that bores the mountain, that stops the wind, that moves
the clouds, that cover the sun, that melts the snow,

that breaks the paw of a little ant going to Jerusalem.
The dog said, "The stick that beats me is stronger than I."
Oh, stick how strong you are, to beat the dog, that chases the cat,
that eats the rat, that bores the mountain, that stops the wind, that moves
the clouds, that cover the sun, that melts the snow,
that breaks the paw of a little ant going to Jerusalem.
The stick said, "The fire that burns me is stronger than I."
Oh, fire how strong you are, to burn the stick, that beats the dog,
that chases the cat, that eats the rat, that bores the mountain,
that stops the wind, that moves the clouds, that cover the sun,
that melts the snow,
that breaks the paw of a little ant going to Jerusalem.
The fire said, "The water that quenches me is stronger than I."
Oh, water how strong you are, to quench the fire
that burns the stick, that beats the dog, that chases the cat,
that eats the rat, that bores the mountain,
that stops the wind, that moves the clouds,
that cover the sun, that melts the snow,
that breaks the paw of a little ant going to Jerusalem.
The water said, "The man that drinks me is stronger than I."
Oh, man how strong you are,
to drink the water that quenches the fire,
that burns the stick, that beats the dog, that chases the cat, that eats the rat, that
bores the mountain, that stops the wind, that moves the clouds that cover the sun,
that melts the snow, that breaks the paw of a little ant going to Jerusalem.
And the man said, "The GOD who made *me* is stronger than I."
Oh, GOD how strong you are,
to make the man, that drinks the water,
that quenches the fire, that burns the stick, that beats the dog,
that chases the cat, that eats the rat,
that bores the mountain, that stops the wind, that moves the clouds,
that cover the sun, that melts the snow,
that breaks the paw of a little ant going to Jerusalem.

A favorite folk tale passed down in the Lathan family.
My dad, Cecil Lathan,
has told this story to me since I was a little girl.

Vickie and Marion Lathan

Realizing your poems are what true poetry should be-
expressions of the heart;
there is one poem you could not fully express because you did not have
the experience of having a sister.

"My Sister"

Written by Marion Lathan, my brother

I wish I could say that I remember the first time your face I beheld
But I have not a memory of those first days, not even a yell
However, there is one thing, as time is changing my hair
I remember of you my dear sister,
No time in my life when you were not there
I've been so blessed to have just known you
By the light that you share from our Lord
But seeing Him in you doesn't come easy
You've prayed and have His spirit and His sword
I pray that His words will flow from your pen
And be seen by the eyes of the world
And see God's rich blessings upon each dear one
Each man, woman, boy and girl
Such joy to be used as His instrument
And I pray that you continue His work
For His words of love are needed so desperately
In this world that's much worse than berserk

My Friend, Katie

Since you became my closest friend some thirty years have passed
This is the kind of friendship that's simply made to last
I hold the memories deep inside of times I spent with you
You're the friend who always knew exactly what to do
You see, we've had a lot in common from the very start
You simply filled a little place down deep within my heart
From small hometowns, to college days and families that care
You see, I found a friendship that I consider rare
You always seem to find the words I really need to hear
They always seem to linger on and wipe away the fear
The times we shared both good and bad
have helped our friendship grow
Today I want to share with you and really let you know
When God sent you to be my friend He picked you from the rest
And now I know He truly sent the very, very best!

Love to You Always

> The godly give good advice to their friends:
> The wicked lead them astray.
> Proverbs 12:26 NLT

Kay Barnes Stewart Crapps

Billy Foxx

Friends

Written for Billy Foxx

How nice it is to be around a friend who always dwells
On the simple little things of life he never seems to fail
To mention how you look today or how he's truly blessed
He always seems to find in one, the very, very best
If it's joy you seek today, I know he'll pass the test
He gives away the joy God gives and helps you find the rest
He can't help but mention how Jesus died that day
And on that cross he took our sins so we may never pay
It's Christ you need, you'll find the rest if only you believe
God's greatest sacrifice came down for you to receive
And if a friend you seek today- what better way to find
A friend who always finds the best and never seems to mind
I know I've found a friend in you, God led me this to say
I thank Him for our friendship each and every day

But the fruit of the Spirit is love, joy, peace, patience,
kindness, goodness,
faithfulness, gentleness and self-control.

Galatians 5: 22 NIV

Tonya Kaiser Moore

Chorus Memories

Written for Tonya Moore

So many have talents but few choose to use
The gifts God has given so we may not lose
God's given these talents to lift up His name
It's not about money nor fortune or fame
When God is our source, His strength He will share
We only must trust Him and cast every care
It's not in our power but God's mighty hand
That helps us to serve Him when we take a stand
Now lives have been touched by how you have shared
The spirit God gave you showed others you cared
The love of the music came straight from the heart
As lives were enriched right from the start

Now bonds were created no one can replace
May God bless your future as daily you face
Always remember you've taught things that last
Reflect on the good times and treasure the past
I pray God will guide you as you journey on
And always remember you're never alone!

> Sing to him a new song;
> play skillfully,
> and shout for joy.
> Psalm 33:3 NIV

Angela Kerr Fluck

Missing You

Written for Angela Kerr

Just to let you know you're missed
No one can take your place
When you're not here, please have no fear
I miss your smiling face
I miss each day the words you say
And how they make me feel
I guess that means our friendship is very, very real!
I pray the Lord will care for you
And guide you through each day
He'll bring you peace and comfort, now this I can say
Please know you're in my thoughts today
No matter where you are
And when you're in my heart you see
That's really not too far.......

I Love You

Every time I think of you,
I give thanks to my God.
Philippians 1:3 NLT 2007

Margaret Lathan Phillips

A Tribute to Aunt Margaret

Margaret Lathan Phillips

Today I'd like to recognize someone who takes the time
To make each one feel special and never seems to mind

She always seems to cater to our every need
And when we come to visit, she always has to feed

I think back to days gone by and how it used to be
As we visited Granny Lathan and sat on Pappy's knee

You see our love for summer started many years ago
As we watched him plant the garden and some even learned to hoe

I think the family's favorite was the corn that Granny made
And now Aunt Margaret is the cook and memories cannot fade

Aunt Margaret you're the glue that keeps our family strong
You always seem to be there when anything goes wrong

And may I simply mention that your stickies pass the test
I'm sure we all agree that they have to be the best!

And if it's corn or cantaloupe, tomatoes or green beans
I'm sure the "Lathan" family can grow the best you've ever seen

You see Granny and Pappy have long since left this place
But in each son and daughter, you can clearly see their face

Thank you God for family who love and care for me
But most of all for Jesus who died to set me Free!

I have not stopped giving thanks for you,
remembering you in my prayers.
Ephesians 1: 16 NIV

Beautiful

Respectful

Intelligent

Talkative

Thoughtful

Assistive

Natural

Youthful

April 5th

November 16th

Dogs: Howie and Maggie

Zackaroo

Amicable

CPA

Kind

Brittany Marie Foster and
Zachary Leigh McCorkle
were married on April 30, 2011.

Mother of the Groom

Kristen, Marion, Cecil, Brittany, Zack, Vickie, Al and Kimberley

Happy Anniversary

April 11, 2008, we met for our very first date
It was dinner at Outback Steakhouse and I could hardly wait
I didn't know what to expect and you probably felt the same
All I had to go on were a few facts and just a simple name
I do remember sitting there, all dressed in black you see
And you were quite a gentleman as I could plainly see

You talked of all your travels and told me of things you've done
We spent about four hours having lots and lots of fun
You walked me to my car that night and we set our next date
You'd come to Olive Garden and help me *celebrate*
And the rest is history as we began to date
I've learned a lot and finally found my true soul mate
And yes, we've celebrated and even shed some tears
But I guess that's expected as we travel through the years

You've done so much to help me and I love you more each day
I hope this helps you realize just what I'm trying to say
Al Strong you've made a difference in my life and many more
I guess next year will be *anniversary number four!*

I Love You

Vickie and Al

Chester Park

*Written for Chester Park Elementary
July 2, 2000*

As we raise our voices Chester Park we sing of you
With gratitude and thanks for everything you do

As we work together let us strive in every way
To make our school a better place, each and every day

We are one, together, as we work in harmony
We are one, together, as we pledge our loyalty

May we always remember every child has special needs
And may each one along the way help this tiny seed

We are one, community and teachers hand in hand
We are one, together, as we take a mighty stand

We all can make a difference but first we must believe
Within the walls of this dear school each one can succeed

We are one-------We are one-------
Together we are one

**This poem was written and later turned into the school song.
Mrs. Jo Ann Wishert wrote the music and
Ms. Vickie McCorkle wrote the words.**

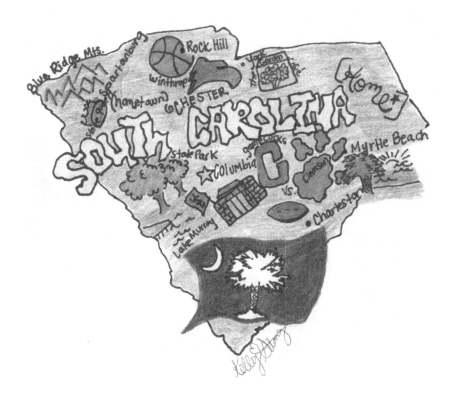

South Carolina

South Carolina

I often think about the place I've always called my home
You see, South Carolina is a wonderful place to roam
From beautiful sandy beaches to a peaceful mountain scene
I'm sure you'll find this state of ours the prettiest you've ever seen
To visit our state capital, to Columbia you must go
And when you visit U.S.C., I'm sure that it will show
What an awesome place it is, you'll never be the same
Just visit Williams-Brice and see every football game

And if you haven't heard about "the" game of the year
Just listen as the crowd cheers out
"Go Gamecocks" have no fear!
Now Tiger fans feel quite the same
They love their team so dear
But once again you'll hear that phrase
Just wait until next year!
Rock Hill is nice, you'll have to choose to come and spend the day
For basketball, you'll have to see the Winthrop Eagles play
If you like to reminisce, then Charleston is for you
Just visit, take a carriage ride and shop the market too!
And if you're looking for good food, I simply recommend
The Garden Cafe, up in York, you'll want to take a friend
And friendly faces you will find in Chester my hometown
And don't forget our State Park, it's the best around
And if it's beauty that you seek, Lake Murray is the best
Just relax, enjoy the view and try to get some rest
Now Spartanburg is responsible for finding the state queen
This could be the hardest job that you've ever seen
For many years girls have come from counties all around
Hoping just to walk away with the precious crown
I hope somehow this helps you find a place to spend the day
Just think about the words above and what I have to say
South Carolina will always be a special place to me
I can't imagine any place that I would rather be!

"Miss Chester"
1976

Vickie Lathan

University of South Carolina 1976-1979

"Home" in Chester
Artwork by Marilyn Pressley

Enjoy God's Gift of Life!

In Loving Memory of...

Hannah Floyd
(December 8, 1986 - December 26, 2010)

McKenzie Mathias
(January 15, 1999 – May 28, 2011)

Stacey McKeown
(December 2, 1974 – June 9, 2011)

Collin Truesdale
(March 14, 1989 – June 14, 2011)